Africa's Changing Geography

by Lillian Duggan

Editorial Offices: Glenview, Illinois • Parsippany, New Jersey • New York, New York
Sales Offices: Needham, Massachusetts • Duluth, Georgia • Glenview, Illinois
Coppell, Texas • Ontario, California • Mesa, Arizona

ISBN: 0-328-13659-X

4 5 6 7 8 9 10 V0G1 14 13 12 11 10 09 08 07 06

Africa

You've waited a long time for this trip. Finally, the huge ocean liner sets sail from New York City. The Statue of Liberty fades in the distance as the ship heads southeast across the Atlantic Ocean. You try to visualize what awaits you at your final destination, the great continent of Africa.

Africa—where humans took their first steps, where the great pyramids of Egypt rise from the desert, and the ancestral homeland for millions of Americans.

With a land area of about 11,724,000 square miles, Africa is more than 2 million square miles larger than North America. Africa contains many kinds of landforms. On your trip you might visit a tropical rain forest, an arid desert, a grassy savanna, or even a snowcapped mountain peak. In this book, we'll look at how geology and climate have shaped the geography you might encounter on a trip to Africa.

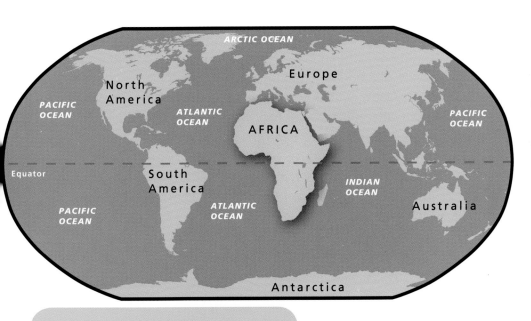

Africa is located south of Europe, between the Atlantic and Indian Oceans.

Geographical Features

On a trip to Africa, you could visit the world's longest river as well as its largest desert. The Nile River, in eastern Africa, is more than 4,000 miles long! And the huge, dry **expanse** of the Sahara spans most of the northern part of the continent.

To the south of the Sahara lie the Sahel and the savanna. The Sahel is a region of dry grassland that receives little rainfall. The savanna is a large, grassy plain that gets more rain than the Sahel.

Africa also has other deserts, including the Namib and the Kalahari in the southern part of the continent.

But Africa is more than a land of dry deserts and grasslands. It is also home to tropical rain forests. The major rain forests sit on the equator. They are home to hundreds of species of both plant and animal life.

Sometimes geographers call Africa the "plateau continent." That's because a huge plateau covers most of Africa. In fact, in much of your trip through Africa, you would be at least 1,000 feet above sea level.

Within the plateau are huge basins, or depressions. These basins—the Djouf, Chad, Sudan, Congo, and Kalahari—are each more than 625 miles across. Each basin, except the Chad, is home to a complex river system.

Africa also has several mountain ranges, including the Atlas Mountains in the northwest, the Ahaggar Mountains in the Sahara, and the Drakensberg Range in the south. Most of Africa's mountains are volcanic, including Mount Kilimanjaro, Africa's highest mountain, at 19,340 feet.

As you travel through Africa, you might wonder how all these geographic features came to be. Read on to find out.

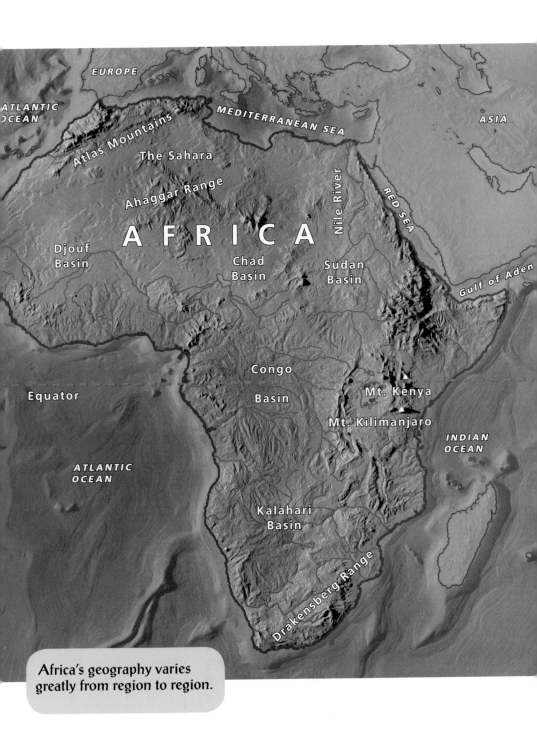

EUROPE

ATLANTIC
OCEAN

MEDITERRANEAN SEA

ASIA

Atlas Mountains

The Sahara

Ahaggar Range

Nile River

RED SEA

A F R I C A

Djouf
Basin

Chad
Basin

Sudan
Basin

Gulf of Aden

Congo
Basin

Mt. Kenya

Equator

Mt. Kilimanjaro

INDIAN
OCEAN

ATLANTIC
OCEAN

Kalahari
Basin

Drakensberg Range

Africa's geography varies
greatly from region to region.

Pangaea

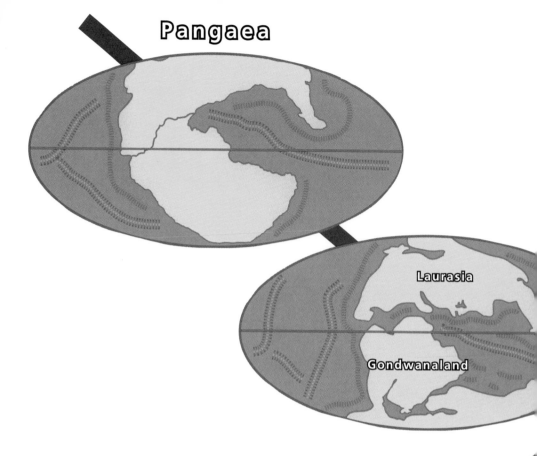

How Africa Was Formed

Scientists believe that all seven of Earth's continents used to be part of one supercontinent named Pangaea. Pangaea had two major sections: Laurasia was made up of North America, Europe, and northern Asia. Gondwanaland included Antarctica, Australia, southern Asia, South America, and Africa.

It seems almost unbelievable, but scientists have good reason to think that Pangaea really existed. They have found evidence that all the continents were once connected; layers of rock found underground in northern Africa closely resemble rocks found in Europe. The Atlas Mountains in northern Africa are an extension of the Alps in southern Europe. And, if you look at a globe, you can see that the coastlines of eastern South America and western Africa fit together, like puzzle pieces.

Around 160 million years ago, Pangaea began to break up. Gradually, South America, Antarctica, Australia, India, Iran, and Southeast Asia broke away from Africa and Arabia. The island of Madagascar also split off from Gondwanaland at that time.

Then Arabia began to break away from the eastern side of Africa. This created the Gulf of Aden and the Red Sea, leaving only a small piece of land connecting Africa to Asia. This piece of land was called the Isthmus of Suez, and it later became the site of the Suez Canal. Built in 1869, the Suez Canal connects the Mediterranean Sea with the Red Sea.

The crack that created the Red Sea also extends on land. On land this crack, or rift, created great rift valleys known as the East African Rift System.

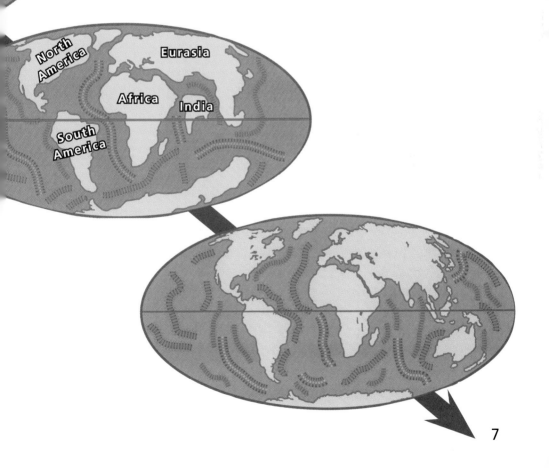

The East African Rift System

At a length of 4,000 miles, the East African Rift System is one of the longest rifts on Earth. It begins in Jordan in southwestern Asia and slices south through eastern Africa, ending in Mozambique.

The main branch of the East African Rift System is the Great Rift Valley, or Eastern Rift Valley. It has an average width of 30 miles, but at its widest point the valley spans 60 miles. To the west of the Great Rift Valley lies the Western Rift Valley.

If you were to climb up from either valley, you would face slopes with an average height of 2,000–3,000 feet. In some places, cliffs drop more than 6,000 feet to the valley floor!

The widest space between the two rifts contains Lake Victoria. When the two rifts first formed, the edges were pushed up and out. A depression formed between them. It filled with water and became Lake Victoria. It is the world's second largest freshwater lake, but Lake Victoria is far less deep than the other rift valley lakes.

Some sections of the rifts have filled with water, forming deep lakes. The largest is Lake Tanganyika. With a length of about 420 miles, it is the longest freshwater lake in the world. It also has a maximum depth of 4,800 feet—that's nearly a mile.

The formation of the East African Rift System also caused magma, or molten rock, to rise from below Earth's surface. The rising magma formed several volcanoes that are found along the rift, two of which are Mount Kilimanjaro and Mount Kenya.

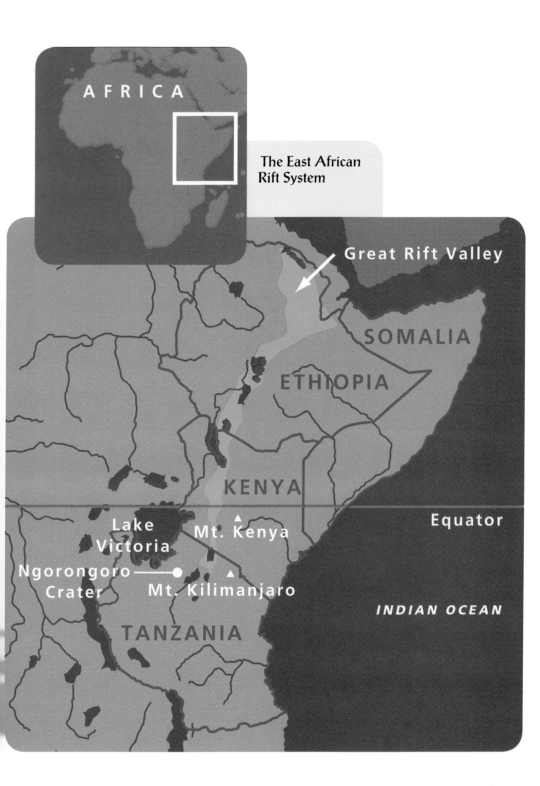

AFRICA

The East African Rift System

Great Rift Valley

SOMALIA

ETHIOPIA

KENYA

Equator

Lake Victoria

Mt. Kenya

Ngorongoro Crater

Mt. Kilimanjaro

INDIAN OCEAN

TANZANIA

Mount Kilimanjaro

Africa's tallest mountain looks as though it arose from nowhere. Where did this lone mountain come from? Mount Kilimanjaro, like other volcanoes, was formed by the gradual buildup of magma that rose to the surface, cooled, and turned to rock.

Perhaps you might miss the cool winter weather back home as you travel through Africa. No need to worry—just climb the mountain. Even though Kilimanjaro lies only two hundred miles north of the equator, it is so high that it is topped with snow.

Kilimanjaro is actually made up of three volcanoes—Kibo, Shira, and Mawenzi. Together, they form a single mountain that is more than fifty miles wide. Kibo is the highest cone of the three, and it is the only one that still occasionally spits hot gases.

Many plants and animals live on Mount Kilimanjaro. Elephants, buffalo, eland (a type of antelope), several species of monkeys, and many types of birds are found in its forests.

The Europeans who first saw Mount Kilimanjaro in the 1800s were shocked to find a snowcapped mountain so close to the equator.

Ngorongoro Crater

To the west of Mount Kilimanjaro, along the Great Rift Valley, sits Ngorongoro. Scientists believe that the crater was formed about 2.5 million years ago, after the cone of an extinct volcano collapsed. This collapse left behind a flat area surrounded by a raised rim. The crater measures 10–12 miles across and has an area of 102 square miles. The rim rises 2,000 feet above the crater's floor.

After millions of years, the crater floor is now open grassland. It is home to elephants, black rhinoceroses, leopards, buffalo, zebras, warthogs, wildebeests, and gazelles. The world's **densest** population of lions lives within the crater, as well.

Ngorongoro Crater also holds a lake—Lake Magadi. Because of the volcanic ash deposited on the lakebed, Lake Magadi's water is alkaline. If you should visit the lake, you will see large flocks of pink flamingoes feeding there.

Ngorongoro Crater is home to the densest population of lions in the world.

The Great Escarpment

After the rest of Pangaea separated from Africa, crust movements forced part of southern Africa to lift. The lift created an elevation known as the Great Escarpment. An escarpment is a long cliff or steep slope separating two, more level, surfaces—one at a lower elevation than the other.

The Great Escarpment is where Africa's plateau ends in the southern part of the continent. In addition, rivers running through some sections of the Great Escarpment have carved gorges into the rock.

If you should decide to visit the Great Escarpment, watch your step . . . it's a long way down!

About 2,000 years ago, the San, or Bushmen, lived in the area of the Great Escarpment and other parts of South Africa. Their rock paintings have been found on the **eaves** of hills in the Great Escarpment.

At the top of the Great Escarpment is the edge of the plateau that covers much of Africa.

The Atlas Mountains

If you were to make your way back from the Great Escarpment in southern Africa to the northwestern part of the continent, you could visit the Atlas Mountains. The Atlas Mountains are actually two mountain chains that run parallel to each other. The two chains, or ranges, developed in different ways and at different times.

The Saharan Atlas is older than its sister mountain range, the Tell Atlas. The Saharan Atlas was formed more than 66.4 million years ago, as a result of the folding, or bending, of Earth's crust. Like the Great Escarpment, the Saharan Atlas is part of the vast plateau that makes up much of Africa.

The Tell Atlas was formed over time between 66.4 and 1.6 millions years ago. First, a group of bent layers of rock, known as folds, raised up over a valley. Then, sheets of sandstone and clay deposits slid down from the north over the rim of the folds, building up the mountain range. Movement beneath the Tell Atlas indicates that the range is still forming today.

The Atlas Mountains separate the Sahara from the shores of the Mediterranean.

The Sahara

If you are the adventurous type, you might turn south and visit the largest desert in the world, the Sahara. It covers a total area of three-and-a-half million square miles—almost the size of the United States. It lies between the Atlas Mountains to the north and the Sahel to the south, and it stretches from the Atlantic Ocean to the Red Sea. The Sahara varies in distance north to south, ranging between 800 and 1,200 miles.

Even though the Sahara is famous for its large seas of sand, only about one-fourth of the great desert is covered with sand dunes. Other parts consist of bare, rocky, or gravelly plains—or even mountains. In fact mountains seem to rise out of nowhere. One of these is Mount Koussi, which, at 11,204 feet, is the highest point in the Sahara.

Like all deserts, the Sahara is very dry. Some regions receive as little as one-quarter of an inch of rainfall in an entire year, while others may not have rain for several years. But the Sahara is not completely dry. Scattered oases, areas where it is wet enough to grow plants, get up to 16 inches of rain per year. An oasis is a welcome sight to thirsty travelers who have **ventured** across the Sahara.

In spite of the dry conditions and difficult terrain, two and a half million people live in the Sahara. That is about one person per square mile.

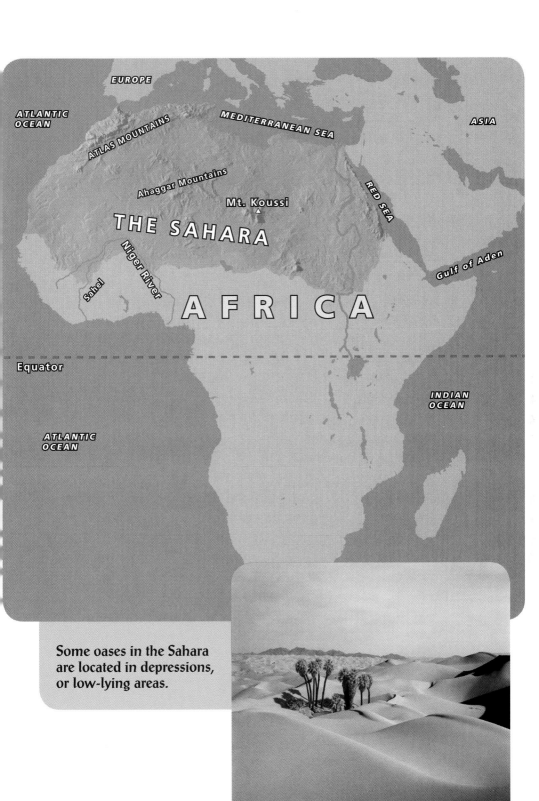

EUROPE

ATLANTIC
OCEAN

MEDITERRANEAN SEA

ASIA

ATLAS MOUNTAINS

Ahaggar Mountains

Mt. Koussi

RED SEA

THE SAHARA

Niger River

Sahel

Gulf of Aden

A F R I C A

Equator

INDIAN
OCEAN

ATLANTIC
OCEAN

Some oases in the Sahara
are located in depressions,
or low-lying areas.

The Sahara's Green Past

You might have a hard time imagining the Sahara as being anything other than a desert. But in fact, the Sahara did not become a desert until about five million years ago. Since then, the Saharan climate has changed from time to time. At times the desert has been more humid, and at other times it has been drier.

Between 5,000 and 10,000 years ago, the Sahara experienced its most recent wet period. Ancient rock art showing images of hippopotamuses indicates that the Sahara must have been wet year-round at one time, because hippos need water constantly.

The Sahara became wet and green because of the shifting of the African monsoon. A monsoon is a wind that can bring tremendous rainfall. Monsoons move both north and south. The movement is affected by the tilt of Earth and the nearness of Earth to the sun.

When the Northern Hemisphere tilts sharply toward the sun and Earth is closest to the sun, Earth receives increased amounts of sunlight. This extra sunlight can cause the African monsoon to shift to the north, dropping rain on dry regions like the Sahara.

About 10,000 years ago, the African monsoon moved into the Sahara, changing the environment of the desert. Then, 5,000 years later, the monsoon moved back toward the south again. After the land dried, it could no longer hold **moisture,** even when it did rain.

However the last wet period in the Sahara left large aquifers beneath the barren landscape. Aquifers are areas of fresh water found underground among rock, sand, or gravel. Today, people mine these aquifers to provide water for farming and drinking.

The Sahara Today

Even today, the Sahara is constantly changing, and the force of wind is a major factor. Strong winds that last for days carry sand, soil, and dust for miles. When these substances are moved from one place to another, the landscape changes in both places.

In the Sahara, winds move in regular patterns. In the north, the wind shifts the sand from west to east. In the south, the sand is shifted from east to west.

Besides causing the sand to shift, winds in the Sahara also mold rock formations. In rocky sections of the Sahara, the wind sculpts yardangs. Yardangs are large sections of rock that are carved by the wind into shapes that are wider at the top than at the bottom. If you were to visit the Sahara, you would find yardangs mainly in the eastern part of the desert.

Other changes taking place in the Sahara and the Sahel to the south threaten the people who live there. For centuries, farmers have grazed their animals on grasses that grow in the Sahel.

However, since the 1960s, the average rainfall in the region has declined. Today, the Sahara appears to be moving south into the Sahel, and Sahel farmers are finding less food for their animals. Some scientists believe that overgrazing is the cause of the drying up of the Sahel. Others feel that an increasingly dry regional climate is to blame.

This yardang in the Sahara was formed by wind.

The Nile River

The Nile River is 4,132 miles long—the longest river in the world. It begins south of the equator and flows north to the Mediterranean Sea.

The Nile has more than one source. The three main streams that feed the Nile are the Blue Nile, the Atbara, and the White Nile. However, Lake Victoria is considered to be the main source of water for the Nile River.

The Nile River basin is the area of land that drains into the Nile. It makes up about one-tenth of the total area of the continent. Several important ancient civilizations developed in this region, because there was enough water to farm along the banks, and the river was a good source of transportation.

Scientists believe that 30 million years ago, the Nile was much shorter. They are not sure how the Nile reached its current length. According to one theory, water from a part of eastern Africa once drained into Lake Victoria. Around 25,000 years ago, some of this water started to shift to a lake to the north. Gradually, material in the water began to collect in that northern lake, causing the lake's water level to rise. The lake began to overflow. The overflow water drained farther to the north and formed its own riverbed. This riverbed linked the southern and northern sections of the Nile and lengthened the river.

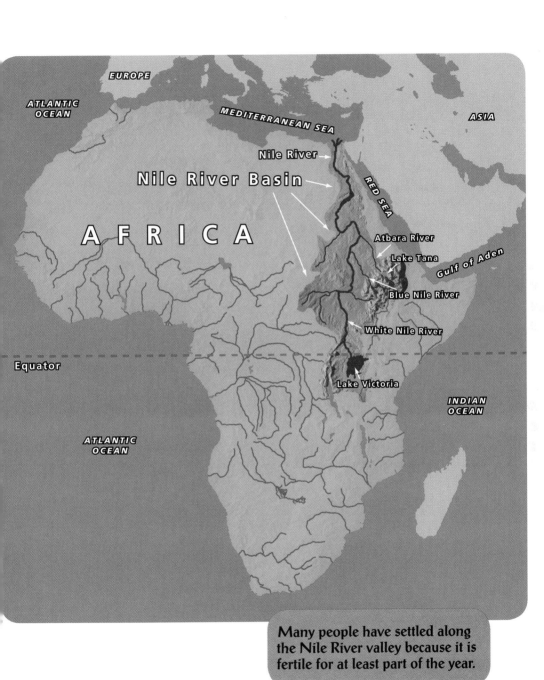

EUROPE

ATLANTIC OCEAN

MEDITERRANEAN SEA

ASIA

Nile River

Nile River Basin

RED SEA

AFRICA

Atbara River

Lake Tana

Gulf of Aden

Blue Nile River

White Nile River

Equator

Lake Victoria

INDIAN OCEAN

ATLANTIC OCEAN

Many people have settled along the Nile River valley because it is fertile for at least part of the year.

The tropical climate in the Nile River valley has played an important role in its geography and agriculture. In the past, annual floods during the summer caused the water level of the river to rise and overflow its banks. In general, people who lived along the Nile welcomed the floods. The floods brought moisture and healthy soil to an area that otherwise could not be farmed.

But the floods could also be dangerous. For centuries, the timing of the flooding of the Nile and the amount of water it would bring could not be predicted. In some seasons, the floods were so severe that they damaged crops growing near the river. There were also occasional droughts.

In 1970, the Aswan High Dam was built in Egypt. The dam makes it possible to control the amount of water that floods the Nile River in most of Egypt, so that farming can be more successful.

Summary

Your imaginary trip through Africa has come to an end. Think about what you have learned about the geologic and climatic causes of change that affect Africa's geography:

- Africa has undergone great changes since it first broke off millions of years ago from the supercontinent, Pangaea.
- Geologic forces are responsible for the formation of huge landforms and entire regions, such as Mount Kilimanjaro, the Great Escarpment, and Lake Victoria.
- Africa's climate, for better or worse, has had a dramatic effect on the Sahara, the Sahel, and the Nile River valley.
- All of these changes, both past and present, are important to the people of Africa, as they try to exploit the resources of that great continent.

Glossary

densest *adj.* the most of something in a given area

eaves *n.* edges of a roof that extend beyond the building

expanse *n.* a large area of something spread out

moisture *n.* water in liquid or vapor form

ventured *v.* to have done something regardless of the risk involved